Unit 4

 HOUGHTON MIFFLIN HARCOURT
School Publishers

Contents

Beep! Beep!

by George Laurents
illustrated by Dave Klug

Dan and his mom went shopping on Main Street. Dan was jog, jog, jogging along. Dan stopped jogging to look in a shop window. Then he and his mom went in to get a good look.

Dan spotted something new in this
shop. Dan and his mom had gone in this
shop last week and had not seen it.

It was big and golden, and it shined
and gleamed. It beeped and beeped on
and off and on.

"Pleased to meet you. Beep, beep, beep. Pleased to meet you. Beep, beep, beep," said the big golden robot.

That speaking and beeping made Dan smile. That speaking and beeping made his mom smile.

Then the robot stopped speaking and beeping, and it began spinning. It spun and spun and then it stopped.

It was as still as a stick. Dan and his mom were quite surprised.

The robot began clapping and humming a song Dan had sung.

"If you are happy and you know it, clap your hands," sang Dan.

"That's fantastic!" exclaimed Mom.

"You like that robot so much, don't
you?" asked his mom.

"I do. Don't you?" asked Dan.

"Yes," agreed his mom. "I was
stunned when it spoke, beeped, clapped,
and hummed."

"Mom, look at that!" exclaimed Dan.

Dan and his mom saw shelf after shelf filled with little gold robots standing still. Then a robot on one shelf began spinning and a robot on another shelf began clapping. Dan was stunned.

Dan's mom asked how much little robots cost. She paid and then handed a robot to Dan. Dan was glad that he had that little robot. Dan, his mom, and his robot went home.

We Helped

by Suzanne Martinucci

I help Nell kick. Nell is learning to kick. She must not bend her leg when she is striking this bag. I help Nell until her kicking is just right. She kicked and kicked. Nell likes kicking and striking.

9

I help children sing songs. I teach
them by strumming notes on strings
and singing. We smile as we sing. We
sing songs each day. Children think that
singing is fun.

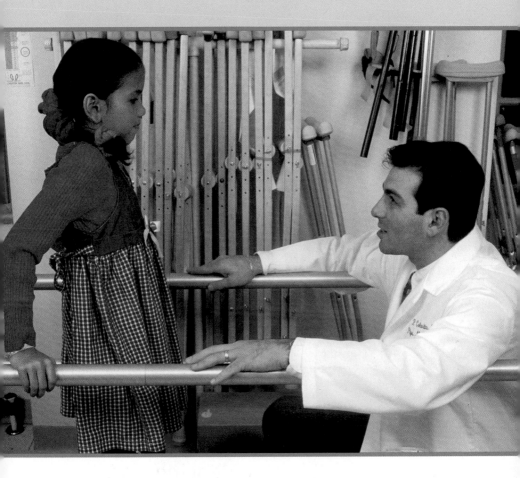

I helped Beth jog. Beth had weak legs.
Beth was afraid of tripping, but she did
not trip. Beth is not afraid of tripping
now. Jogging helped Beth. It made her
legs strong. Beth did well!

I help children in dancing class. Children begin class with skipping and hopping. Then I help Joan and Tess with standing and stretching. Joan and Tess hold on and stretch their legs. They keep their legs still.

I help Greg ride his brand new bike.
I can help him stay on and keep his
balance. Greg will need a nice wide space
to ride in. Greg thinks sitting on his bike
and riding is fun. We have gone biking
each day this week.

I help Ben play. When Ben is sitting,
I tell Ben how to hold the bow. Ben can
play scales, but Ben likes playing tunes.

Ben played tunes on a big stage.
Everyone clapped and said that Ben
played well.

I help plants grow. Growing plants
need sun, water, and food. Growing
plants need space as well.

If a plant grows too big for its pot, I
dig it up. After digging, I put it in a big
pot so it can keep growing.

I helped Jane and held her hand as she stepped down. She had to take her time.

Stepping down steps is something Jane likes. Helping Jane stay safe makes both Jane and me glad.

Bright Lights

by Paul Enoch

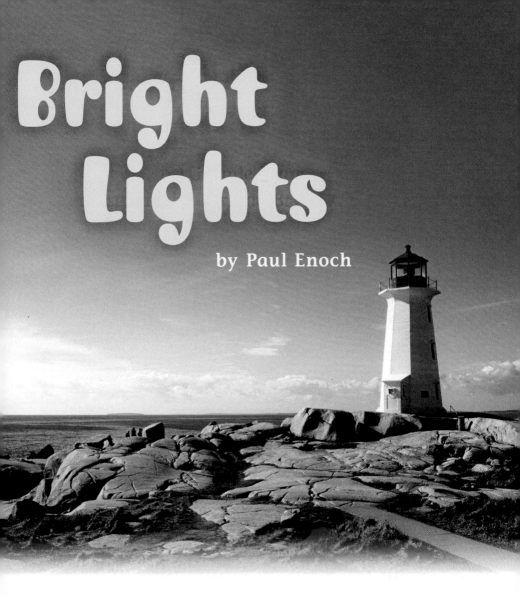

This is a lighthouse. It has a big light in it. At night, that big light shines. It is a bright, bright light.

This light is why people made
lighthouses. At night, people on ships
might not see where land is. Land might
have just a few dim lights. People on
a ship must see lights or else that ship
might bump right into land and rocks.

At night, people on ships can see this bright light sent by the lighthouse. This bright light tells them not to get near that lighthouse. This big, bright light helps ships. It makes sure that ships stay safe at sea.

Try to find the light on this lighthouse. When this light is doing its job, bright lights go on and off. It sends red light, then white light. Red, white, red, white, red, white, go the lights.

This lighthouse has white stripes.
These white stripes show in daytime.
People on ships can see these stripes then.
At night, bright light shines. People can
find this lighthouse by day and by night.

People who ride on a ship might see
this by day. They can see this lighthouse.
Its big light is high up so it can be seen.
The ship is not near it. The ship is safe.
It is safe by day and by night.

People who ride on a ship might see this by night. They can see just bright light. They can not see much land at night. They just see that big bright light at night. The ship is safe. It is safe.

People like to visit an old lighthouse. They like to go by day and by night. Why? Can it be because its bright light tried to keep ships safe by day and by night? Is that why?

Wild Cats

by Jean Deacon
illustrated by Philomena O'Neil

"Wake up, Mom!" cried Ly. "It is time to get up. Rise and shine, Mom!"

"Yes," said Mom. "I can see that the sun is up. Sunlight will light our path."

25

Mom and Ly began their long trip. Ly and his mom went to find Wild Cat Path. This path was made by wild cats. Many kinds of wild cats use this path. It goes up in the high hills.

"Mom, is this the right path?" asked
Ly. "Did we find it?"

"Yes," said his mom. "I am sure this
path is the right path. It will take us up
high in the hills."

Ly and his mom went on. Bright
sunlight did light this wild path. Ly was
silent for a while.

"Let's play 'I Spy,'" said Ly.

"That's fine with me," said his mom.
"You go first."

"I spy someone nice and kind," said Ly.
"Is it that red bug?" asked Mom.
"No," said Ly.
"Is it that green insect?" asked Mom.
"No, it's my mom," said Ly. "You are
someone nice and kind."

Mom said, "I spy someone who is fun
to be with."

"Is it the black fly on that green vine?"
asked Ly.

"No," said Mom.

"Is it that tan pine bug?" asked Ly.

"No," said Mom. "It is not."

Ly was silent for a while.

"What else can I ask? Is it me, myself?" asked Ly.

"That's right, Ly! That's right," said Mom. "You are fun to be with."

Ly and Mom went high up on Wild Cat Path. The end was in sight.

"See what those cats are doing? Might you try that?" asked Mom.

"I sure will," cried Ly. "I can jump high, high, high! I am sure!"

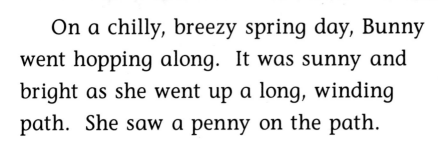

Bunny and the Penny

by Emily Banks
illustrated by Bernard Adnet

On a chilly, breezy spring day, Bunny
went hopping along. It was sunny and
bright as she went up a long, winding
path. She saw a penny on the path.

Bunny held the shiny penny. She can get a treat for her mom with this penny. What will she get? She will ask other mothers to help her plan.

Bunny needs help. Maybe Nanny Goat can help Bunny.

34

"I need help, Nanny Goat. What can I get my mom with my shiny penny?" Bunny asked.

"You can get a cherry and a berry," said Nanny Goat. "Yummy treats!"

"Thanks," Bunny cried.

Bunny hopped along and then stopped.
"Maybe I can get a treat Mom might
like more than a cherry and a berry,"
Bunny thought. "I will ask Patty Pony.
She might help me."

"I need help, Patty Pony. What can
I get my mom with my shiny penny?"
Bunny asked.

"Get oats and hay," Patty Pony said.

"Thanks," Bunny cried.

Bunny hopped along, happy that her
friends had tried to help.

"Maybe I will see a treat that Mom
will like more than oats and hay," Bunny
thought.

Bunny hopped into The Penny Shop.

Bunny saw the words "Huge Green
Leafy Plant for Sale."

"Yummy! Yummy!" yelled Bunny.

Bunny handed Sandy Pig her shiny
penny. Sandy Pig handed Bunny the
huge green leafy plant.

Bunny rushed home.

"This is for you!" Bunny cried.

"This is a fine, yummy treat. It is just the right treat for me. How did you know?" Mom asked.

"I asked other mothers, but this was my own plan," Bunny beamed.

"Yummy! Yummy!" Mom cried.

Puppies

by Stuart MacNeil

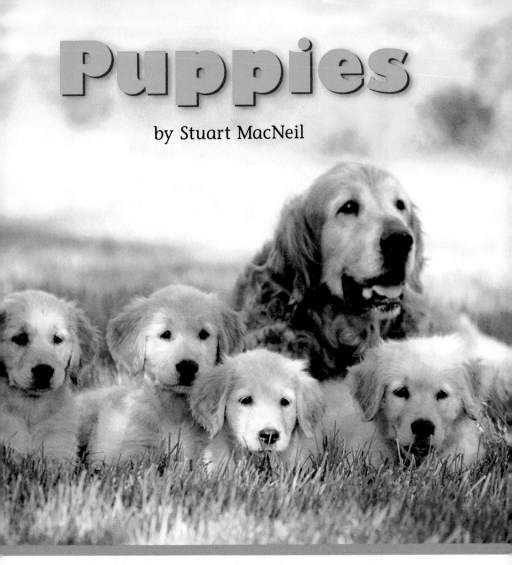

Puppies are so cute! Just look at these happy little golden puppies!

Mothers of puppies take care of them and help them grow.

41

People may have puppies as pets.
Jenny carries this tiny puppy. Which
words might Jenny use when she tells
about her puppy? Would she say it is
sweet? nice? sleepy?

To keep puppies well, people take them
for checkups at the vet. This vet will
check to see if this puppy has a thick coat
and strong teeth. He will see if the puppy
is growing and if it is happy.

In cities, people find grassy places
where puppies can play. This black puppy
likes this grassy place. He can sniff at
daisies growing in the grass.

At the beach, people take puppies to play by the sea. This puppy is safe on his leash as he watches the waves. The wet mud feels so cold on his feet.

What do puppies like? These kids
think puppies like wagon rides. Nancy
tries to pull this wagon. It carries two of
her friends and three puppies.

Sometimes puppies hide. This red box
is a fine hiding place.

Each fluffy puppy peeks out. What
can these puppies see? They can see you!

Puppies play a lot, but puppies need sleep. Sleep helps puppies grow.

Puppies have soft, warm bodies. When it's naptime, these sweet puppies stay close to each other and take cozy naps.

Sometimes starlings have small white spots. Starling spots are like stars or snowflakes.

Darling has a large white spot just above her eye. This large white spot tells which dark starling is Darling.

Darling has two pals. Marty and Arnie are her best friends. These three starlings start each day together.

Today, Darling, Marty, and Arnie meet at the city park at sunrise. All these friends greet each other by cheeping, "Cheep, cheep, cheep."

"We can fly to Park Arch today,"
cheeps Marty. "I'll start."

"Let's fly," cheeps Arnie.

"Let's go," cheeps Darling.

"Follow me," cheeps Marty. Then with
three flip, flap, flaps, all three starlings
fly up like the wind.

"Look, Marty. Look, Darling. Park Arch is not so far now," cheeps Arnie.

"Right! I'll land at Park Arch," cheeps Marty.

"Then I will land with Marty," cheeps Darling.

"I'll land with you," cheeps Arnie.

"Let's march around Park Arch,"
cheeps Darling.

"Please, let me start. I'll lead this
march and you follow," cheeps Arnie.

"March on!" cheeps Marty.

"March, 2, 3, 4," cheeps Arnie.

"March, 2, 3, 4," cheeps Darling.

Darling, Marty, and Arnie keep
marching, but Bart Lark stops them.

"Please come to my party," sings Bart
Lark. "My party is starting right now."

"We will," cheep the starlings. "We
will." The party didn't stop until the
park got dark.

Going to the Farm

by Matt Lloyd
illustrated by Ana Ochoa

Marge and Carl had never been on a farm. Their home is in Star City. Marge and Carl lived high up, far above Star City streets.

In March, Marge and Carl got an
e-mail. Gram and Gramps sent it. This
e-mail asked Marge and Carl to visit
Gram and Gramps on May 30. It said,
"Please stay until school starts."

"That's a 90 day visit," said Marge.

"It's a far trip. How can we get that far?" asked Carl.

"We can go by plane," said Dad. "I'll make plans so we can go."

The next day, Marge, Carl, and Dad
went to the park.

"What will we do on the farm?"
asked Marge.

"We can send an e-mail and ask Gram
and Gramps," said Carl.

Marge and Carl sent an e-mail to
Gram and Gramps. The next day, Dad
showed Marge and Carl an e-mail.

"It's from Gram and Gramps," he said.
"They sent nice snapshots as well. I'll
show them to you."

Dad read the e-mail:

"We are so glad you will be visiting us. This is our barn. Cows live inside this barn. Sheep live outside. Sheep roam around inside their fence. Sheep can get inside if it is cold."

"This cow's name is Marta. You can help us milk Marta. This sheep's name is Barb. We use Barb's white fleece to make white yarn. We will see you on May 30! Love, Gram, Gramps, Marta, and Barb."

"I'll start packing!" said Marge.

"Not yet, Marge," said Carl. "We go on May 30. It's still March!"

"I didn't think of that," said Marge. "I'm just so happy we get to go! I will mark that date!"

A · Sporty · Game

by Cindy Harmon
illustrated by Emma Stevenson

This sunny spring morning, Mort
wore a red top, tan shorts, and a
sporty yellow cap.

"I look so sporty," he said. "This is
a fine day for playing a sport and I am
ready. I am ready to play."

Mort grabbed his golf club and
hopped off his porch. He rode his bike
and beeped his horn to greet Luke. Luke
sat on his porch dressed in a yellow top,
green shorts, and sporty red cap.

"This is a fine day for a sport. Can you play golf with me at Golf Park?" Mort asked.

"I've been waiting to be asked," said Luke. "See my golf club? I am set. Let's get going."

Mort and Luke rode along Shore
Road until they came to Golf Park.
It was just the sort of place Mort and
Luke liked. It had nine golf holes.
The grass was fresh and green.

Mort hit the ball. It went under the mill and came out. With three more short strokes, the ball fell in that hole. Luke hit five strokes for that hole. Five strokes!

The sky got dark and a sudden
rainstorm began. It rained with such
force that everyone ran and waited
for that rainstorm to end. They did not
want to get wet.

Well, not everyone ran. Mort
stayed and hit the ball by a sand
trap. Then he hit it in the hole. Luke
hit five short strokes before he got
the ball in.

"Such a nice day for a sporty golf game," yelled Mort, as rain dripped on his face.

"Yes," sighed Luke. "It is such a nice day. Just the sort of day we like being at Golf Park."

Mort and Luke played on until the very last hole.

My Story

by Shawn Dibbs
illustrated by Jeff Shelly

I like to write stories. I've filled notebooks with short stories that I wrote. Here is a sports story that I hope you like reading.

Before I begin, I must say that
I am a real Jays fan. The last game
was just the sort of game that keeps
fans going back to see more and more
games. I am just that sort of fan.

That game was being held at Shore
Gym. I wore a hat with jays on it and
shorts with jays on them.

The Jays and Sharks played. Both
were fine sports teams.

   With just a short time left, the score
was tied 16 to 16. Fans sat still.

   Ray hit a short shot into the net and
Sharks fans jumped up clapping and
cheering. That made the score Sharks 18
and Jays 16.

Ken shot for the Jays, but Cort came running, ready to block his shot. Cort grabbed the ball and shot it with great force right into the net.

Fans clapped for Cort. The score was Sharks 20 and Jays 16.

It seemed that the Jays would not win this game. Then, Greg tried a very long shot. Fans gasped when that ball hit the rim, then spun, and dropped in the net. It was three more for the Jays, making the score Sharks 20 and Jays 19.

The silent fans sat still. No clapping!
No cheering! The scores were so close,
and not much time was left. Chuck had
the ball for the Sharks, but as he tried a
shot, he lost the ball. Pat picked it up for
the Jays. What next?

Would Pat make that shot?

Yes!

Pat tossed the ball and it dropped in.
A horn beeped and the game ended. The
Jays had 21 and the Sharks had 20.

As I said before, I am a real Jays
fan. I was so happy being at the game
that day.

Word Lists

Accompanies
Mr. Tanen's Tie Trouble

Beep! Beep!

page 1

Decodable Words
Target Skill: *Base words and endings -ed, -ing, including doubling final consonant and /ed/, /t/, /d/ pronunciations for -ed*
agreed, asked, beeped, beeping, clapped, clapping, exclaimed, filled, gleamed, handed, hummed, humming, jogging, pleased, shined, shopping, speaking, spinning, spotted, standing, stopped, stunned, surprised

Words Using Previously Taught Skills
along, and, as, at, beep, began, big, clap, cost, Dan, don't, fantastic, get, glad, golden, had, hands, he, his, home, if, in, it, jog, last, like, made, Main, meet, mom, much, not, on, paid, quite, robot, robots, sang, seen, she, shelf, shop, smile, so, song, spoke, spun, stick, still, Street, sung, that, that's, then, this, week, went, when, window, with, yes

High-Frequency Words
New
gone, said, something

Previously Taught
a, after, another, are, do, good, happy, how, I, know, little, look, new, off, one, saw, the, to, was, were, you, your

We Helped

page 9

Decodable Words
Target Skill: *Base words and endings -ed, -ing, including doubling final consonant and /ed/, /t/, /d/ pronunciations for -ed*
biking, clapped, dancing, digging, growing, helped, helping, hopping, jogging, kicked, kicking, learning, played, playing, riding, singing, sitting, skipping, standing, stepped, stepping, stretching, striking, strumming, tripping

Words Using Previously Taught Skills
afraid, and, as, bag, balance, begin, Ben, bend, Beth, big, bike, both, bow, brand, but, can, children, class, day, did, dig, each, fun, glad, Greg, grow, grows, had, hand, held, help, him, his, hold, if, in, is, it, its, Jane, Joan, jog, just, keep, kick, leg, legs, likes, made, makes, me, must, need, Nell, nice, not, notes, on, plant, plants, play, pot, ride, safe, scales, she, sing, smile, so, songs, space, stage, stay, steps, still, stretch, strings, strong, sun, take, teach, tell, Tess, that, them, then, think, thinks, this, time, trip, tunes, until, up, we, weak, week, well, when, wide, will, with

High-Frequency Words
New
gone, said, something

Previously Taught
a, after, by, down, everyone, food, for, have, her, how, I, new, now, of, put, right, the, their, they, to, too, was, water

82

Bright Lights

page 17

Decodable Words

Target Skill: *Long i spelled i, igh, ie, y*
bright, by, find, high, light, lighthouse, lighthouses, lights, might, night, right, tried, try, why

Words Using Previously Taught Skills

an, and, at, be, because, big, bump, can, day, daytime, dim, get, go, has, helps, in, is, it, its, job, just, keep, land, like, made, makes, much, must, not, old, on, red, ride, rocks, safe, sea, see, seen, sends, sent, shines, ship, ships, show, so, stay, stripes, tells, that, them, then, these, this, up, visit, when, white

High-Frequency Words

New
doing, else, sure

Previously Taught
a, few, have, into, near, off, or, people, the, they, to, where, who

Wild Cats

page 25

Decodable Words

Target Skill: *Long i spelled i, igh, ie, y*
bright, by, cried, find, fly, high, I, kind, kinds, light, Ly, might, my, myself, right, sight, silent, Spy, sunlight, try, wild

Words Using Previously Taught Skills

am, and, ask, asked, be, began, black, bug, can, Cat, cats, did, end, fun, get, go, green, hills, his, in, insect, is, it, it's, jump, let's, long, made, me, mom, nice, no, not, on, path, pine, play, red, rise, see, shine, sun, take, tan, that, that's, this, those, time, trip, up, us, use, vine, wake, we, went, what, while, will, with, yes

High-Frequency Words

New
doing, else, sure

Previously Taught
a, are, first, for, goes, many, of, our, said, someone, the, their, to, was, who, you

Bunny and the Penny

page 33

Decodable Words

Target Skill: *Long e sound for y*
berry, breezy, Bunny, cherry, chilly,
happy, leafy, Nanny, Patty, penny,
Pony, Sandy, shiny, sunny, yummy

Words Using Previously Taught Skills
along, and, as, ask, asked, bright,
can, cried, day, get, Goat, green, had,
handed, hay, held, help, hopped,
hopping, huge, I, it, like, long, maybe,
me, might, mom, my, needs, oats, on,
path, Pig, plan, plant, Sale, see, she,
Shop, spring, stopped, than, thanks,
that, then, this, treat, treats, tried, up,
went, will, winding, with, yelled

High-Frequency Words

New
friends, mothers, words

Previously Taught
a, for, her, into, more,
other, said, saw, the,
thought, to, was, what,
you

85

Puppies

page 41

Decodable Words

Target Skill: *Base words and endings -s, -es, changing y to i*
bodies, carries, cities, daisies, puppies, tries

Target Skill: *Long e sound for y*
cozy, fluffy, grassy, happy, Jenny, Nancy, puppy, sleepy, tiny

Words Using Previously Taught Skills
and, as, at, beach, black, box, but, can, care, check, checkups, close, coat, cold, cute, each, feels, feet, find, fine, golden, grass, grow, growing, has, he, help, helps, hide, hiding, his, if, in, is, it, it's, just, keep, kids, leash, like, likes, lot, may, might, mud, naps, naptime, need, nice, on, peeks, pets, place, places, play, red, rides, safe, say, sea, see, she, sleep, sniff, so, soft, stay, strong, sweet, take, teeth, tells, them, these, thick, think, this, three, use, vet, wagon, watches, waves, well, wet, when, which, will

High-Frequency Words

New
friends, mothers, words

Previously Taught
a, about, are, by, do, for, have, her, little, look, of, other, out, people, pull, sometimes, the, they, to, two, warm, what, where, would, you

Darling Starling

page 49

Decodable Words
Target Skill: *r-controlled vowels ar*
Arch, Arnie, Bart, dark, Darling, far,
large, Lark, march, marching, Marty,
park, party, sharp, starling, starlings,
stars, start, starting

Words Using Previously Taught Skills
and, are, as, at, be, beaks, best, but, by,
can, cheep, cheeping, cheeps, city, day,
each, eat, feet, flap, flaps, flip, fly, follow,
go, got, greet, has, I, is, just, keep, land,
lead, let, let's, life, like, likes, me, meet,
my, not, on, pals, play, rain, right, she,
shiny, sings, snowflakes, so, spot, spots,
stop, stops, sunrise, tells, them, then,
these, this, three, until, up, we, well,
which, white, will, wind, with

High-Frequency Words
New
didn't, I'll, please

Previously Taught
a, above, all, around, come,
eye, friends, have, her, look,
now, or, other, small, some,
sometimes, the, they, to,
today, together, two, you

Going to the Farm

Decodable Words

Target Skill: *r-controlled vowels ar*
Barb, Barb's, barn, Carl, far, farm,
March, Marge, mark, Marta, park, Star,
start, starts, yarn

Words Using Previously Taught Skills

an, and, as, ask, asked, be, by, can,
City, cold, cow's, cows, Dad, date, day,
e-mail, fence, fleece, from, get, glad, go,
got, Gram, Gramps, had, happy, help,
high, home, I, I'm, if, in, inside, is, it, it's,
just, make, May, milk, name, next, not,
on, packing, plane, plans, read, roam,
see, send, sent, sheep, sheep's, show,
showed, snapshots, so, stay, still, streets,
that, that's, them, think, this, trip, until,
up, us, use, visit, visiting, we, well, went,
white, will, yet

High-Frequency Words

New
didn't, I'll, please

Previously Taught
a, above, are, around, been,
do, how, live, never, of, our,
said, school, the, their, they,
to, what, you

A Sporty Game

page 65

Decodable Words

Target Skill: *r-controlled vowels or, ore*
for, force, horn, more, morning, Mort, porch, rainstorm, Shore, short, shorts, sort, sport, sporty, wore

Words Using Previously Taught Skills
along, am, and, asked, at, be, beeped, before, began, bike, by, came, can, cap, club, dark, day, did, dressed, dripped, end, face, fell, fine, five, fresh, game, get, going, golf, got, grabbed, grass, green, greet, had, he, his, hit, hole, holes, hopped, I, in, is, it, just, last, let's, like, Luke, me, mill, my, nice, nine, not, on, Park, place, playing, rain, rained, ran, red, Road, rode, sand, sat, see, set, sighed, sky, so, spring, stayed, strokes, such, sudden, sunny, tan, that, this, three, top, trap, until, waited, waiting, want, we, well, went, wet, with, yelled, yellow, yes

High-Frequency Words

New
being, I've, ready

Previously Taught
a, ball, been, everyone, look, of, off, out, said, the, they, to, under, very, was, you

89

My Story

Decodable Words

Target Skill: *r-controlled vowels or, ore*
before, Cort, for, force, horn, more,
score, scores, Shore, short, shorts, sort,
sports, stories, story, wore

Words Using Previously Taught Skills

am, and, as, at, back, beeped, begin,
block, both, but, came, cheering, Chuck,
clapped, clapping, close, dropped,
ended, fan, fans, filled, fine, game,
games, gasped, going, grabbed, Greg,
Gym, had, happy, hat, held, his, hit,
hope, I, is, it, jays, jumped, just, keeps,
Ken, last, left, like, long, lost, made,
make, making, much, must, net, next,
no, not, notebooks, on, Pat, picked,
played, Ray, reading, real, right, rim,
running, sat, say, see, seemed, Sharks,
shot, silent, so, spun, still, teams, that,
them, then, this, three, tied, time, tossed,
tried, up, when, win, with, wrote, yes

High-Frequency Words

New
being, I've, ready

Previously Taught
a, ball, great, here, into,
look, of, off, out, said, the,
to, very, was, were, what,
would, write, you